STUDY GUIDE

Kingdom Feast

Coming to the Lord's Table

R.C. Sproul

LIGONIER MINISTRIES
Renew your Mind.
LIGONIER.ORG | 800-435-4343

421 Ligonier Court, Sanford, FL 32771
E-mail: info@ligonier.org

Printed in the United States of America.

1

The Significance of the Passover

MESSAGE INTRODUCTION

The institution of the sacrament of the Lord's Supper did not occur in a historical vacuum. The Lord's Supper was instituted in the middle of the traditional Jewish Passover. This Old Testament feast was central to the worship of Israel, and Jesus gave it an entirely new meaning. He Himself became the Passover Lamb. In this lecture, Dr. Sproul examines the origin and meaning of the Old Testament Passover in order to provide the context for understanding the meaning of the Lord's Supper.

LEARNING OBJECTIVES

1. To be able to explain the historical context behind the institution of the Passover
2. To be able to explain the points of connection between the Passover and the Lord's Supper

QUOTATIONS

And the Lord said to Moses and Aaron, "This is the statute of the Passover: no foreigner shall eat of it, but every slave that is bought for money may eat of it after you have circumcised him. No foreigner or hired worker may eat of it. It shall be eaten in one house; you shall not take any of the flesh outside the house, and you shall not break any of its bones. All the congregation of Israel shall keep it. If a stranger shall sojourn with you and would keep the Passover to the Lord, let all his males be circumcised. Then he may come near and keep it; he shall be as a native of the land. But no uncircumcised person shall eat of it."

—Exodus 12:43–48

Your boasting is not good. Do you not know that a little leaven leavens the whole lump? Cleanse out the old leaven that you may be a new lump, as you really are unleavened. For Christ, our Passover lamb, has been sacrificed.

—1 Corinthians 5:6–7

LECTURE OUTLINE

A. Introduction

1. At the very heart of the life and worship of the early Christian community was the celebration of the Lord's Supper, and throughout history this sacrament has been known by several names.
2. Members of the early church used to celebrate what they called an "agape feast," or a love feast, in which they celebrated the love of God and their love for one another in this holy supper.
3. The sacrament has also been called the "Lord's Supper" because of its reference to the Last Supper that Jesus had with His disciples on the night before His death.
4. The sacrament has been referred to as "Holy Communion" because of the emphasis on our mystical union and communion with Christ in the Supper.
5. The Lord's Supper also became known early on as the "Eucharist" because this is the Greek word that means "to thank," and the Supper was seen as a time when the people of God gathered to express their gratitude for what Christ had accomplished on their behalf.

B. The Passover Context of the Lord's Supper

1. The Lord's Supper is a drama that has its roots not only in the Upper Room experience that Jesus shared with His disciples, but also in the Old Testament Passover.
2. Jesus instituted the Lord's Supper during the celebration of the Passover on the night before He died.
3. The link between Christ's death and the Passover is also seen in Paul's writings when he says, "Christ, our Passover, was sacrificed for us."
4. The Passover story begins with the enslavement of the people of Israel in Egypt.
5. The Israelites cried out to God, who heard their cry and called Moses to the task of delivering the people out of bondage.
6. At God's command, Moses went before Pharaoh and told him to let the people go.
7. A power struggle between God and Pharaoh ensued, and God sent several plagues upon Egypt.
8. The tenth plague was the worst in that it involved the death of the firstborn sons of all the Egyptians.
9. In the context of the declaration of this tenth plague, God institutes the Passover.
10. Each Israelite family was to sacrifice an unblemished lamb, place its blood on the door of their house, and eat its roasted flesh with bitter herbs—all while dressed and ready to leave at a moment's notice.
11. God would pass over the houses marked with the lamb's blood, sparing them from death.

C. Saved From What?

1. People often ask, "Are you saved?"
2. A good response is, "Saved from what?"

3. The term *to save* means a number of things in Scripture.
4. The ultimate meaning of the term *saved* in Scripture is "to be saved from the ultimate calamity—falling under the wrath of God."
5. We are not only saved *by* God; we are also saved *from* God.
6. The idea of being saved from God is dramatically displayed in the Old Testament Passover feast.
7. In the New Testament, Jesus changes the Passover and indicates that His blood will now mark those to be saved from the wrath of God.

STUDY QUESTIONS

1. Which term for the sacrament of the Supper reflects its emphasis on the giving of thanks to God?
   a. The Eucharist
   b. The agape feast
   c. The Lord's Supper
   d. Holy Communion

2. Which term for the sacrament of the Supper reflects its emphasis on our mystical union and communion with Christ in the Supper?
   a. The Eucharist
   b. The agape feast
   c. The Lord's Supper
   d. Holy Communion

3. What Old Testament feast provided the context for the institution of the Lord's Supper?
   a. Hanukkah
   b. Passover
   c. Pentecost
   d. Purim

4. In preparation for the Passover meal, what animal were the Israelite families commanded to sacrifice?
   a. A bull
   b. A lamb
   c. A goat
   d. A dove

BIBLE STUDY

1. Read Exodus 12:1–51, and answer the following questions:
   a. Why is it significant that God tells Moses that this Passover will be the beginning of a new calendar for Israel?

b. Is the Passover ceremony centered on individuals or on families?
c. What principal things does God command the Israelites to do in preparation for the Passover?
d. Does the Passover distinguish between the act of sacrifice and the sacrificial meal? If so, is the eating of the lamb the act of sacrifice or the sacrificial meal? Is this distinction significant? If so, why?
e. How are future generations of Israelites to participate in this great act of redemption?
f. What prerequisite for participation in the Passover is emphasized repeatedly in 12:43–48?

2. Read Matthew 26:2, 17–19; Mark 14:1, 12, 14, 16; and Luke 22:1, 7, 8, 11, 13, 15. How do these texts prove that the Lord's Supper was instituted during the celebration of the Passover?

3. In 1 Corinthians 5:6–7, Paul refers to Christ as "our Passover" who was sacrificed for us. What is the significance of this statement in light of what the Old Testament says about Passover?

DISCUSSION QUESTIONS

1. Explain the basic features of the Old Testament Passover. What was involved? Who was involved? What did they do?
2. The Passover was a communal, family-oriented sacrament of the old covenant. What significance, if any, does this have for our understanding of the Lord's Supper?
3. Does the book of Exodus clearly indicate whether young children partook of the Passover meal? Is there any sense in which young children participated in the sacrament of Passover simply by virtue of the fact that they were in a house marked by the blood of the Passover lamb? What relevance might your answers have in the debate over whether young children should be permitted to partake of the Lord's Supper?

APPLICATION

1. Reflect on what it means to be saved from the wrath of God, to have God's judgment pass over you. The next time you partake of the Lord's Supper, give thanks (Eucharist) to God for marking you with the blood of the Lamb and sparing you from His judgment and wrath.
2. Take the time to study Exodus 12 in depth. Find a good commentary on Exodus (for example, Currid or Mackay) and discover what this feast meant to the Jews and why Jesus strongly desired to partake of it with His disciples.

FOR FURTHER STUDY

Calvin, John. *Institutes of the Christian Religion*, 4.17
Currid, John D. *Exodus*, 2 vols.
Mackay, John L. *Exodus*
Mathison, Keith. *Given for You: Reclaiming Calvin's Doctrine of the Lord's Supper*, chapters 5–6
Nevin, John Williamson. *The Mystical Presence: A Vindication of the Reformed or Calvinistic Doctrine of the Holy Eucharist*
Sproul, R.C. *What Is the Lord's Supper?*
Wallace, Ronald. *Calvin's Doctrine of Word and Sacrament*

2

The Institution of the Lord's Supper

MESSAGE INTRODUCTION

All people mark special times for remembrance. We celebrate birthdays and wedding anniversaries because of the significance of those occasions in our lives. In instituting the Lord's Supper, Jesus marked a special point in time and told His disciples to remember it by observing the sacrament of the Supper. In this lecture, Dr. Sproul examines the memorial nature of the Lord's Supper.

LEARNING OBJECTIVES

1. To be able to explain how the Lord's Supper is related to the past dimension of time
2. To be able to outline some of the reasons why people mark sacred time

QUOTATIONS

Now as they were eating, Jesus took bread, and after blessing it broke it and gave it to the disciples, and said, "Take, eat; this is my body." And he took a cup, and when he had given thanks he gave it to them, saying, "Drink of it, all of you, for this is my blood of the covenant, which is poured out for many for the forgiveness of sins. I tell you I will not drink again of this fruit of the vine until that day when I drink it new with you in my Father's kingdom."

—Matthew 26:26–29

As the apostle teaches that the rock from which spiritual drink sprang forth for the Israelites was Christ [1 Cor. 10:4]—because it was a visible sign under which that spiritual drink indeed truly was, but was not discernible to the eye—so the body of Christ today is called bread, inasmuch as it is the symbol by which the Lord offers us the true eating of his body.

—John Calvin

LECTURE OUTLINE

A. Introduction

1. The formal institution of the Lord's Supper took place in the upper room on the night before Jesus' crucifixion.
2. Luke's account of the institution of the Supper is found in chapter 22, verses 7–22 of his gospel.

B. Past, Present, and Future

1. In Luke's description of the institution of the Lord's Supper, we see Jesus make explicit reference to two dimensions of time.
2. The way we generally measure the passing of time in our culture is by referring to the past, the present, and the future.
3. When we look at the meaning of the Lord's Supper in the life of the Christian community, we see that the Supper is related to all three dimensions of time.

C. The Lord's Supper as a Memorial of Sacred Time

1. The Lord's Supper is related to the past by virtue of its link to the Passover.
2. It is also linked to the past in that what Jesus asked His disciples to remember is now past to us.
3. We see frequently in redemptive history what we would call the "sacralization" of space and time.
4. In other words, we see countless examples of God or Israel giving sacred significance to particular times or places in this world.
5. When God spoke to Moses from the burning bush (Exodus 3), He instructed Moses to remove his shoes because the ground was holy ground.
6. After the floodwaters receded, Noah built an altar to God to consecrate and memorialize the place where God had delivered him and his family from the deluge (Genesis 8:20).
7. The festivals of the Old Testament involved the sacralization of time.
8. The Passover, as we have seen, memorialized the redemption of the people of Israel from slavery in Egypt.
9. There are also sacred days in the church calendar that celebrate the birth of Christ, the death of Christ, the resurrection of Christ, and other major events in biblical history.
10. Each Lord's Day is, in fact, a sacred day.
11. People want to remember those moments that are most important for their salvation.
12. Jesus understood the link between forgetting and apostasy, knowing that the very word *apostasy* means "a letting go of or forgetting."
13. An apostate is someone who has forgotten that to which he was once committed.
14. There are some who want to reduce the entire significance of the Lord's Supper to one of remembrance, but the Lord's Supper has a present and future aspect as well.

STUDY QUESTIONS

1. The formal institution of the Lord's Supper took place ____________.
   a. When Jesus gave the Great Commission
   b. During the Olivet Discourse
   c. In the upper room on the night before Jesus' crucifixion
   d. During Jesus' crucifixion

2. The word ____________ means "a letting go of or forgetting."
   a. Sacralization
   b. Apostasy
   c. Memorialization
   d. Heresy

BIBLE STUDY

1. Matthew 26:17–25 provides the context for the institution of the Lord's Supper, the record of which is found in verses 26–30. Read verses 17–25. On what day does Jesus tell His disciples to prepare the Passover meal? How are Passover and the Feast of Unleavened Bread related, according to Exodus 12–13? What is the first major announcement that Jesus makes during the observance of the meal itself?
2. Read Matthew 26:26. What four things did Jesus do with the bread? What two things does He tell the disciples to do with the bread? What does Jesus say about the bread? Normally, the Passover liturgy would include the following words: "This is the bread of affliction which our ancestors ate when they came from the land of Egypt." Is it reasonable to suppose that the Jews who used these words believed they were eating the very pieces of bread that their ancestors had eaten and digested? Is it more reasonable to suppose that the Jews used this language to point to their own real participation in the act of redemption that their ancestors had experienced firsthand? How does our understanding of the words used in the normal Passover liturgy help in our understanding of Jesus' words about the bread?
3. Read Matthew 26:27–29. What does Jesus say about the cup of Passover wine in these verses? How do Exodus 24:8; Jeremiah 31:31–34; and Isaiah 53:12 shed light on our understanding of Jesus' words? How do Jesus' words point to an eschatological, or future, aspect of the Lord's Supper?
4. Read Matthew 26:30. At the end of the Passover meal, the Jews would sing Psalms 115–118. Read these Psalms slowly and carefully, and note the words that were being sung by Jesus as He prepared to go to Gethsemane and ultimately to the cross. Do any of the words of these psalms stand out when we know that Jesus sang them as He faced the prospect of death?

DISCUSSION QUESTIONS

1. Should the Christian church set aside certain days in the calendar to remember certain events in Christ's life? Why or why not? Is the celebration of Easter and Christmas appropriate for Christians? Why or why not? How would you respond to the argument that the liturgical calendar, in which certain events in Christ's life are celebrated on specific days, helps us to remember that the events recorded in the Bible happened in real history and that they are not simply myths?
2. According to the Roman Catholic church, if we interpret Jesus' words "This is My body" literally, we must come to the conclusion that the bread is (or becomes) Christ's actual body. How would you evaluate this argument?

APPLICATION

1. Write down some of the special places and times in your life. Which, if any, of these have you memorialized in some special way?
2. Reflect on the major events in redemptive history, including Christ's incarnation, His death, resurrection, and ascension, and Pentecost. Think about why it is important to always remember that these events occurred in real history and involved real people.

FOR FURTHER STUDY

Calvin, John. *Institutes of the Christian Religion*, 4.17
Geldenhuys, Norval. *Commentary on the Gospel of Luke*, pp. 550–60
Lane, William. *The Gospel According to Mark*, pp. 496–509
Letham, Robert. *The Lord's Supper*
Mathison, Keith. *Given for You: Reclaiming Calvin's Doctrine of the Lord's Supper*, chapter 6
Nevin, John Williamson. *The Mystical Presence: A Vindication of the Reformed or Calvinistic Doctrine of the Holy Eucharist*
Sproul, R.C. *What Is the Lord's Supper?*
Wallace, Ronald. *Calvin's Doctrine of Word and Sacrament*

3

The Consummation of the Kingdom

MESSAGE INTRODUCTION

The Lord's Supper does not merely look to something that happened in the past. Jesus also points to the future, promising to once again drink the fruit of the vine with His disciples when the kingdom of God is consummated at the wedding feast of the Lamb. The Lord's Supper is a promise that all who are faithful to Christ will partake of this feast. In this lecture, Dr. Sproul examines the forward-looking aspects of the Lord's Supper.

LEARNING OBJECTIVES

1. To be able to explain how the Lord's Supper is related to the future dimension of time
2. To be able to explain how the Lord's Supper assures the faithful that they will participate in the wedding feast of the Lamb

QUOTATIONS

> *And he took a cup, and when he had given thanks he said, "Take this, and divide it among yourselves."*
>
> —Luke 22:17

> *After this I heard what seemed to be the loud voice of a great multitude in heaven, crying out, "Hallelujah! Salvation and glory and power belong to our God, for his judgments are true and just; for he has judged the great prostitute who corrupted the earth with her immorality, and has avenged on her the blood of his servants." Once more they cried out, "Hallelujah! The smoke from her goes up forever and ever." And the twenty-four elders and the four living creatures fell down and worshiped God who was seated on the throne, saying, "Amen. Hallelujah!" And from the throne came a voice saying, "Praise our God, all you his servants, you who fear him, small and great." Then I heard what seemed to be the voice of a great multitude, like the roar of many waters and like the sound of mighty*

peals of thunder, crying out, "Hallelujah! For the Lord our God the Almighty reigns. Let us rejoice and exult and give him the glory, for the marriage of the Lamb has come, and his Bride has made herself ready; it was granted her to clothe herself with fine linen, bright and pure"—for the fine linen is the righteous deeds of the saints. And the angel said to me, "Write this: Blessed are those who are invited to the marriage supper of the Lamb." And he said to me, "These are the true words of God."

—Revelation 19:1–9

LECTURE OUTLINE

A. The Future Orientation of the Lord's Supper

1. In Luke's account of the Lord's Supper, we read, "And he took a cup, and when he had given thanks he said, 'Take this, and divide it among yourselves. For I tell you that from now on I will not drink of the fruit of the vine until the kingdom of God comes" (Luke 22:17–18).
2. In verses 28–30, Jesus tells His disciples, "You are those who have stayed with me in my trials, and I assign to you, as my Father assigned to me, a kingdom, that you may eat and drink at my table in my kingdom and sit on thrones judging the twelve tribes of Israel."
3. Jesus, the Anointed One whom the Father has declared to be King of kings and Lord of lords, focuses on the future consummation of His kingdom.
4. Jesus promises His disciples that there will be a time in the future when they will sit with Him at His table.

B. Pictures of the Wedding Feast

1. In Psalm 23, David declares, "You prepare a table before me in the presence of my enemies" (v. 5).
2. When God vindicates His people, He vindicates them in the presence of those who have falsely accused them of all kinds of slander.
3. Psalm 23 anticipates the coming of the Messiah as the Good Shepherd.
4. In Matthew 22, Jesus tells the parable of the wedding feast.
5. Christ's coming brings a division between those who reject Him and those who embrace Him.
6. In one sense, this parable is a recapitulation of the history of Israel, the nation invited by God to be His bride, but which rejected Him and refused to come to His wedding feast.
7. God then invites to the feast other people (Gentiles) who were not part of the original community.
8. In Revelation 19:1–9, reference is made to the marriage feast of the Lamb.
9. John is given a glimpse here of what God has in store for His people in the final consummation of His kingdom.

C. The Lord's Supper

1. In the institution of the Lord's Supper, Jesus calls attention to that future time when He will sit down with His people and celebrate the feast of the kingdom of God.
2. Every time we celebrate the Lord's Supper, we do not merely look back to what has already been accomplished by Christ; instead, we realize that although our redemption has been accomplished in history, another chapter remains to be written.
3. We have experienced the inauguration of the kingdom and the coronation of the King of that kingdom, but we still await the final consummation of that kingdom.
4. The Lord's Supper is God's sign and seal of what will happen in the future.
5. The Lord's Supper is a foretaste of heaven where we will see the Bridegroom in all of His glory and will see the church offered to Him in perfection.

STUDY QUESTIONS

1. In which Psalm does David first describe the Lord as a Shepherd and then declare, "You prepare a table before me in the presence of my enemies"?
   a. Psalm 2
   b. Psalm 12
   c. Psalm 23
   d. Psalm 40

2. In which chapter of Matthew does Jesus tell the parable of the wedding feast?
   a. Matthew 12
   b. Matthew 22
   c. Matthew 24
   d. Matthew 26

3. In which one of the following chapters of the Book of Revelation is reference made to the marriage feast of the Lamb?
   a. Revelation 3
   b. Revelation 9
   c. Revelation 17
   d. Revelation 19

BIBLE STUDY

1. Read Matthew 26:29; Mark 14:25; and Luke 22:17–18. In all of these accounts, Jesus announces that He will not eat with the disciples again until the great eschatological banquet. It is worth noting that the cup from which He abstains is the fourth and final cup of the Passover meal. His words indicate that He will not drink the fourth cup until the time of the consummation of the kingdom, at which time He will feast with all the redeemed (see Revelation 19:6–9). Does this

mean that there is some sense in which the Last Supper is unfinished? Does it mean that there is some sense in which the church's ongoing celebration of the Lord's Supper throughout history is really a continued participation in the third cup of that final Passover meal?

2. Read the parable of the wedding feast in Matthew 22:1–14. Outline the major characters and plot developments in this parable. How do these characters and plot developments parallel the story of Israel?
3. Read Revelation 19:1–9. What is being described by John in these verses? Where does the marriage supper of the Lamb fit into this scene?

DISCUSSION QUESTIONS

1. How does an understanding of the structure and order of the Passover meal help us to better understand the meaning and significance of Jesus' words regarding the cup of wine that He will not drink until the kingdom of God comes?
2. In what way does our present participation in the Lord's Supper point us toward that final consummation feast—the marriage supper of the Lamb?
3. What should be our attitude in response to the invitation that we have received to participate in the feast?

APPLICATION

1. Do you ever find yourself exhibiting an attitude toward participating in the Lord's Supper similar to the attitude expressed by the guests initially invited to the king's feast in the parable of the wedding feast? If so, reflect on the meaning of the Supper and partake with thanksgiving and rejoicing.
2. If you are a believer, thank God for inviting you to participate in the marriage supper of the Lamb. Thank Him every time you get a foretaste of this feast in the Lord's Supper.

FOR FURTHER STUDY

Calvin, John. *Institutes of the Christian Religion*, 4.17

Letham, Robert. *The Lord's Supper*

Mathison, Keith. *Given for You: Reclaiming Calvin's Doctrine of the Lord's Supper*

Nevin, John Williamson. *The Mystical Presence: A Vindication of the Reformed or Calvinistic Doctrine of the Holy Eucharist*

Sproul, R.C. *What Is the Lord's Supper?*

Wallace, Ronald. *Calvin's Doctrine of Word and Sacrament*

4

Real Body and Blood?

MESSAGE INTRODUCTION

The Lord's Supper is not only oriented toward the past and the future. It also has a present significance. In fact, most of the controversies over the Lord's Supper in the history of the church have been controversies over the present significance of the Supper. Is Christ somehow really present in the sacrament? If so, how? These questions have been debated for centuries. In this lecture, Dr. Sproul introduces some of the key terms in the debate over the present significance of the Supper.

LEARNING OBJECTIVES

1. To be able to explain the basic Aristotelian categories of *substance* and *accidens*
2. To be able to outline the key points of the way in which Christ's presence in the sacrament was understood by the Roman Catholics, the Lutherans, and John Calvin

QUOTATIONS

The cup of blessing that we bless, is it not a participation in the blood of Christ? The bread that we break, is it not a participation in the body of Christ?

—1 Corinthians 10:16

I conclude, that Christ's body is really, (as the common expression is)—that is, truly given to us in the Supper, to be wholesome food for our souls.

—John Calvin

And the godly ought by all means to keep this rule: whenever they see symbols appointed by the Lord, to think and be persuaded that the truth of the thing signified is surely present there. For why should the Lord put in your hand the symbol of his body, except to assure you of a true participation in it? But if it is true that a visible sign is given us to seal the gift of a thing invisible, when we have received the symbol of the body, let us no less surely trust that the body itself is also given to us.

—John Calvin

LECTURE OUTLINE

A. Introduction

1. We have examined the temporal orientation of the Lord's Supper with respect to the past and also with respect to the future.
2. What about the present significance of the celebration of the Lord's Supper?
3. Most of the controversies that have arisen over the subject of the Supper have been controversies over the present aspect of the sacrament.
4. The majority of the church throughout history has believed in the real presence of Christ in the Supper, so that when we gather at the table we are in real communion with Him.
5. That is about all that the majority agree on because the real issue of dispute has been the mode of Christ's real presence.

B. This Is My Body

1. Part of what is necessary to understand the mode of Christ's presence is an understanding of His words of institution.
2. In the accounts of the Last Supper in all three Synoptic Gospels, Jesus says, "This is my body."
3. The controversy has focused on the meaning of the word *is* in the statement.
4. The word *is* can be used as a copula to indicate strict identity.
5. It can also be used in a metaphorical way to indicate representation.
6. The verb *to be* is used in a metaphorical sense in the "I am" sayings in the gospel of John.
7. The controversy centers on whether the word *is* in the words of institution is being used to indicate identity or to indicate representation.
8. In the first-century Roman community, Christians were being charged with the crime of cannibalism.
9. In the sixteenth century, the Lutherans and the Reformed were unable to find complete unity precisely because of a difference in understanding the meaning of *is* in the words of institution.

C. Transubstantiation

1. One of the major controversies in the sixteenth century had to do with the Roman Catholic understanding of Christ's presence.
2. The Roman Catholic Church taught then, and continues to teach now, the doctrine of transubstantiation.
3. According to the doctrine of transubstantiation, the substance of the bread and wine are supernaturally transformed into the actual body and blood of Jesus.

4. The doctrine is formulated in the way it is because to the five human senses there is no discernible difference in the bread and wine before and after its consecration.
5. In order to account for this problem, the Roman church borrowed metaphysical categories from Aristotle to articulate her doctrine.
6. Aristotle distinguished between the *substance* and *accidens* of a thing.
7. That which makes a thing what it is is the *substance* of a thing.
8. The external, perceivable qualities of a thing are the *accidens*.
9. Aristotle believed that every object had its own substance, and every substance had its corresponding *accidens*.
10. The church said that in the Mass a double miracle takes place.
11. On the one hand, the substance of the bread and wine changes into the substance of the body and blood of Christ while the *accidens* of bread and wine remain the same.
12. Prior to the miracle, what is on the altar is the substance of bread and the *accidens* of bread.
13. After the miracle, what is on the altar is the substance of the body of Christ and the *accidens* of bread.
14. The second miracle, then, is that we have the substance of the body and blood of Christ without the *accidens* of body and blood.
15. Aristotle never allowed for the substance of one thing to exist with the *accidens* of another, but this idea became the official doctrine of the Roman Catholic Church.

D. The Doctrine of the Protestant Reformers

1. Luther objected to the doctrine of transubstantiation because he believed it involved a frivolous miracle.
2. Luther believed that the real flesh of Christ was present in the element of bread, but that it is in, under, and through the element.
3. According to Luther, the bread and wine do not become the body and blood of Christ; instead, the body and blood of Christ are supernaturally added to the bread and wine.
4. Many of the other Reformers, such as Calvin and the Swiss Reformers, rejected Luther's view on christological grounds.
5. In regard to the Lord's Supper, John Calvin fought a battle on two fronts.
6. On the one hand, he disagreed with Zwingli and those who thought that the Lord's Supper was merely a memorial.
7. On the other hand, he disagreed with the Roman Catholics and Lutherans, who thought that Christ's real presence was a physical and corporeal presence.

STUDY QUESTIONS

1. Most of the controversies that have arisen over the subject of the Supper have been controversies over the ____________ aspect of the sacrament.
   a. Past
   b. Present
   c. Future
   d. Pretemporal

2. The Roman Catholic Church officially teaches the doctrine of ___________.
    a. Consubstantiation
    b. Symbolic memorialism
    c. Transubstantiation
    d. Transignification

3. In order to articulate her understanding of the mode of Christ's presence in the Supper, the Roman Catholic Church borrowed metaphysical categories from what philosopher?
    a. Aristotle
    b. Socrates
    c. Plato
    d. Zeno

BIBLE STUDY

1. The following texts all speak of the sacramental elements used in the Lord's Supper *after* any consecration would have taken place. How are the elements described in each of these texts? What significance do these texts have in relation to the debate over transubstantiation?
    a. Matthew 26:29
    b. 1 Corinthians 10:17
    c. 1 Corinthians 11:26, 27, 28
2. The Roman Catholic Church insists that a plain and literal interpretation of Jesus' words of institution naturally leads to the doctrine of transubstantiation. This is based on the assumption that the word *is* in the text be taken to mean literal identity. Does the word *is* (and the other forms of the verb *to be*) in Scripture always indicate strict identity? Examine the following texts of Scripture, and indicate whether the form of the verb *to be* is being used to indicate strict identity or being used metaphorically. Based on your answers, would you say that the grammar alone of Matthew 26:26 can tell us the meaning of the word *is* in the text, or must the meaning of the word be determined by the context?
    a. Mark 3:11
    b. Luke 1:18
    c. 1 Corinthians 9:2
    d. 2 Corinthians 6:16

DISCUSSION QUESTIONS

1. The Roman Catholic Church defines a sacrament as "a symbol of a sacred thing." Does the doctrine of transubstantiation conflict with this definition? If so, how?
2. The Roman Catholic Church teaches the concept of "oral manducation"—the idea that the body and blood of Christ are ingested orally. Thomas Aquinas, and the Roman church following him, teaches that the substance of a thing can be

grasped only by the intellect or the mind. Only *accidens* can be grasped by the senses. Since the doctrine of transubstantiation results in a sacrament in which we are said to have the substance of the body and the blood of Christ with the *accidens* of bread and wine, what is it that can be physically eaten even within the bounds of the Roman doctrine? Can there be an "oral manducation" of substance if Aquinas is correct? Is there a fundamental self-contradiction within the Roman Catholic doctrine at this point?

3. The Roman Catholic Church teaches that Christ's presence in the sacrament is bodily and corporeal. Yet, His presence is also said to be intangible, invisible, and without spatial quantity. If properties such as tangibility, visibility, and spatial quantity are not part of the essential defining characteristics of a corporeal body, then what is the precise difference between a "body" and a "spirit"? Is it self-contradictory to speak of a corporeal presence and then describe that presence in terms that define incorporeal realities?
4. Martin Luther vehemently insisted that Christ's words "This is my body" be taken literally. He therefore proposed the doctrine of consubstantiation, in which the body and blood of Christ are said to be "in, with, and under" the elements of bread and wine. Is the doctrine of consubstantiation a strictly literal interpretation of Christ's words, specifically the word *is*?

APPLICATION

1. Which view of the Lord's Supper have you been taught? Do you see any strengths or weaknesses in this doctrine that you had not noticed before studying this series?
2. What have you learned in this lesson that will help you as you approach the Lord's Table in the future?

FOR FURTHER STUDY

Berkouwer, G.C. *The Sacraments*, pp. 188–201
Calvin, John. *Institutes of the Christian Religion*, 4.17
Keener, Craig S. *A Commentary on the Gospel of Matthew*
Mathison, Keith. *Given for You: Reclaiming Calvin's Doctrine of the Lord's Supper*
Sproul, R.C. *What Is the Lord's Supper?*
Wallace, Ronald. *Calvin's Doctrine of Word and Sacrament*

5

The Natures of Christ

MESSAGE INTRODUCTION

One of the primary objections raised by John Calvin and the Swiss Reformers against the Roman Catholic doctrine of transubstantiation and the Lutheran doctrine of consubstantiation was that both doctrines contradicted the church's doctrine of Christ. More specifically, it was objected that these doctrines contradicted the Definition of the Council of Chalcedon regarding the person of Christ. In this lecture, Dr. Sproul introduces this extremely important issue and explains the heart of the disagreement.

LEARNING OBJECTIVES

1. To be able to outline the basic Chalcedonian definition of Christ
2. To be able to explain how the Roman Catholic and Lutheran doctrines of the Eucharist contradict the Definition of Chalcedon

QUOTATIONS

We, then, following the holy fathers, all with one consent, teach men to confess one and the same Son, our Lord Jesus Christ, the same perfect in Godhead and also perfect in manhood; truly God and truly man, of a reasonable soul and body; consubstantial with the Father according to the Godhead, and consubstantial with us according to the Manhood; in all things like unto us, without sin; begotten before all ages of the Father according to the Godhead, and in these latter days, for us and for our salvation, born of the Virgin Mary, the Mother of God, according to the Manhood; one and the same Christ, Son, Lord, Only-begotten, to be acknowledged in two natures, inconfusedly, unchangeably, indivisibly, inseparably; the distinction of natures being by no means taken away by the union, but rather the property of each nature being preserved, and concurring in one Person and one Subsistence, not parted or divided into two persons, but one and the same Son, and only begotten, God, the Word, the Lord Jesus Christ, as the prophets from the beginning [have declared] concerning him, and the Lord Jesus Christ himself has taught us, and the Creed of the holy fathers has been handed down to us.

—The Definition of Chalcedon

But some are carried away with such contentiousness as to say that because of the natures joined in Christ, wherever Christ's divinity is, there also is his flesh, which cannot be separated from it. As if that union had compounded from two natures some sort of intermediate being which was neither God nor man! So, indeed, did Eutyches teach, and Servetus after him. But from Scripture we plainly infer that the one person of Christ so consists of two natures that each nevertheless retains unimpaired its own distinctive character.

—John Calvin

LECTURE OUTLINE

A. Introduction

1. The primary issue in the debate over the nature of Christ's presence was christological.
2. The issue in question is whether it is possible for the body of Jesus to be present in numerous places at the same time.
3. If the Mass is celebrated at more than one place at a time, and if Christ's actual flesh and blood are present in the elements of the sacrament wherever it is celebrated, then Christ's human nature would have to be present at all of these places at the same time.

B. Early Christological Heresies

1. In AD 451, the Council of Chalcedon dealt with several heresies that were threatening the church's doctrine of Christ.
2. These heresies were coming from two different directions.
3. On the one hand was the Monophysite heresy, which was being taught by a man named Eutyches.
4. The prefix *mono* means "one," and the word *phusis* means "nature" or "substance."
5. According to the Monophysite heresy, Jesus was one person with one nature, and that one nature was a mixture or blending of divine and human attributes.
6. According to Eutyches, Christ had a single "theanthropic" nature.
7. The other heresy that was being advanced was the Nestorian heresy.
8. The Nestorians said that in Christ there were two distinct natures and two distinct persons.
9. The Nestorians separated the divine and human natures into two distinct persons.
10. One heresy was advocating a blending or mixing of the divine and human, while the other was advocating a dividing or separating of the two natures.

C. The Definition of Chalcedon

1. The Council of Chalcedon declared that Christ is truly God and truly man and that He has two distinct natures.

2. The divine nature is truly divine in all that that involves, and the human nature is truly human in all that that involves except for sin.
3. Sinfulness is not a necessary attribute of humanity.
4. The council also attached to its confession what are commonly referred to as the four negatives.
5. The church basically said that it is impossible to define exactly how the two natures are related to each other, but it is possible to name several ways in which they are *not* related.
6. The church declared that the two natures are united without mixture, confusion, separation, or division.
7. The humanity is not swallowed up by the deity, and the deity is not swallowed up by the humanity.
8. Nor can the human nature and divine nature be separated or divided.
9. There is distinction without separation.
10. Immediately after stating these four negatives, the council added the declaration that each nature retains its own attributes.
11. In the incarnation, the divine nature does not cease to be divine, and the human nature does not cease to be human.
12. The kenotic heresy of the nineteenth century argued that Christ emptied Himself of His divine attributes in the incarnation.
13. What Jesus laid aside was His prerogatives to glory.

D. The Doctrine of Ubiquity

1. If the human nature of Christ retains its attributes (including such attributes as spatial limitation), a difficulty arises for those who want to maintain a bodily presence of Christ in the Lord's Supper.
2. Calvin argued that the doctrine of transubstantiation was in clear violation of the church's own Council of Chalcedon.
3. In response, the Roman Catholic Church developed the doctrine of the communication of attributes and the doctrine of ubiquity.
4. *Ubiquity* is simply a synonym for "omnipresence."
5. The Roman church argued that Christ's human nature was ubiquitous by virtue of the communication of divine attributes to the human nature.

STUDY QUESTIONS

1. In AD 451, the Council of____________dealt with several heresies that were threatening the church's doctrine of Christ.
   a. Nicea
   b. Constantinople
   c. Ephesus
   d. Chalcedon

2. According to the ___________ heresy, Jesus was one person with one nature, and that one nature was a mixture or blending of divine and human attributes.
   a. Monophysite
   b. Nestorian
   c. Arian
   d. Docetic

3. Which heresy separated the divine and human natures of Christ into two distinct persons?
   a. The Eutychian heresy
   b. The Nestorian heresy
   c. The Monophysite heresy
   d. The Arian heresy

4. The ___________ heresy of the nineteenth century argued that Christ emptied Himself of His divine attributes in the Incarnation.
   a. Monophysite
   b. Kenotic
   c. Unitarian
   d. Modalist

5. *Ubiquity* is a synonym for ___________.
   a. Holiness
   b. Aseity
   c. Omnipresence
   d. Omniscience

BIBLE STUDY

1. Examine the following passages of Scripture: Matt. 4:2; 26:38; Luke 2:40, 52; John 4:6; 11:35; 12:27; and 19:28. How do each of these texts reveal the truly human nature of Christ?
2. What do the following texts of Scripture teach us about Jesus and sin: 2 Cor. 5:21; Heb. 4:15; 7:26; 1 Pet. 1:19; 2:22; and 1 John 3:5?
3. Examine the following passages of Scripture: John 1:1, 18; 20:28; Acts 20:28; Rom. 9:5; Phil. 2:6; Col. 2:9; 2 Thess. 1:12; 1 Tim. 3:15–16; Titus 2:13; Heb. 1:8; 2 Pet. 1:1; and 1 John 5:20. How do each of these texts indicate the truly divine nature of Christ?
4. How does Matthew 8:24–27 illustrate the distinction between the divine and human natures of Christ?
5. Why is it important that Jesus always refers to Himself as "I" and "Me" rather than "We" or "Us" and that the biblical authors always refer to Him as "He" and "Him" rather than "They" or "Them"?

DISCUSSION QUESTIONS

1. Outline the basic Chalcedonian definition of the person of Christ and explain how it counters the Eutychian and Nestorian heresies.
2. Explain how the Roman Catholic and Lutheran doctrines of the Eucharist contradict the Definition of Chalcedon.

APPLICATION

1. Take the time to study the Definition of Chalcedon, which outlines the orthodox Christian doctrine of the person of Christ. Reflect on the biblical truths that the early church was seeking to protect with this definition.
2. The next time you study the Gospels, note those passages that point to the human nature of Christ, those that point to the divine nature, and those that point to the single person.

FOR FURTHER STUDY

Bray, Gerald. *Creeds, Councils and Christ*
Calvin, John. *Institutes of the Christian Religion*, 4.17
Kelly, J.N.D. *Early Christian Doctrines*
Macleod, Donald. *The Person of Christ*
Wells, David F. *The Person of Christ*

6

The Presence of Christ

MESSAGE INTRODUCTION

John Calvin always insisted that his debate with the Roman Catholics and Lutherans was not over the fact of Christ's real presence in the Lord's Supper but in the manner or mode of that presence. The Roman Catholics and Lutherans were both forced by their theologies to suggest a doctrine of ubiquity that Calvin believed to be in contradiction with orthodox Christology. How, then, did Calvin maintain a doctrine of the real presence of Christ without falling into a similar trap? In this lecture, Dr. Sproul introduces the Reformed doctrine of the presence of Christ in the Lord's Supper.

LEARNING OBJECTIVES

1. To be able to explain why Lutherans accuse those who adhere to the Reformed doctrine of the Lord's Supper of holding to an implicit Nestorianism
2. To be able to provide a brief explanation of how Christ can be said to be present in the Lord's Supper without attributing ubiquity to His human nature

QUOTATIONS

Worthy receivers, outwardly partaking of the visible elements, in this sacrament, do then also, inwardly by faith, really and indeed, yet not carnally and corporally but spiritually, receive, and feed upon, Christ crucified, and all benefits of His death: the body and blood of Christ being then, not corporally or carnally, in, with, or under the bread and wine; yet, as really, but spiritually, present to the faith of believers in that ordinance, as the elements themselves are to their outward senses.

—Westminster Confession of Faith, 24.7

I here embrace without controversy the truth of God in which I may safely rest. He declares his flesh the food of my soul, his blood its drink [John 6:53ff.]. I offer my soul to him to be fed with such food. In his Sacred Supper he bids me take, eat, and drink his body and blood under the symbols of bread and wine. I do not doubt that he himself truly presents them, and that I receive them.

—John Calvin

LECTURE OUTLINE

A. Introduction

1. Sometimes when we look at the mystery of the incarnation, and particularly as we apply it to our understanding of the Lord's Supper, it seems as if we can get hopelessly lost in a maze of confusion.
2. Reformed believers often say that the Lutheran view of the presence of Christ is implicitly Eutychian, while Lutherans often say that the Reformed doctrine is implicitly Nestorian.
3. A correct understanding of the Reformed doctrine of Christ's presence in the sacrament does not lead to Nestorianism.

B. Real Presence versus Physical Presence

1. The Westminster Confession of Faith says the following about the Lord's Supper: "Worthy receivers, outwardly partaking of the visible elements, in this sacrament, do then also, inwardly by faith, really and indeed, yet not carnally and corporally but spiritually, receive, and feed upon, Christ crucified, and all benefits of His death: the body and blood of Christ being then, not corporally or carnally, in, with, or under the bread and wine; yet, as really, but spiritually, present to the faith of believers in that ordinance, as the elements themselves are to their outward senses (24.7)."
2. The confession makes a distinction between the real presence of Christ and the physical presence of Christ.
3. It insists that Christ's presence is a real spiritual presence.
4. The term *spiritual presence* can easily be misunderstood to mean a presence only in the mind or heart, but that is not what the confession is teaching.

C. An Illustration

1. Calvin made an important contribution to the debate with his formula *finitum non capax infinitum.*
2. This statement means, "The finite cannot contain the infinite."
3. In terms of the sacramental debate, it is another way of saying that the human body of Christ is not omnipresent.
4. Calvin also said that those who partake of the Lord's Supper are really strengthened and nurtured by the human nature of Christ, which is made present to us by the divine nature.
5. It may be of some help to provide some illustrations demonstrating how such a concept is possible.

6. First, we can draw a circle that indicates the person of Christ, and there's one circle because there is only one person.

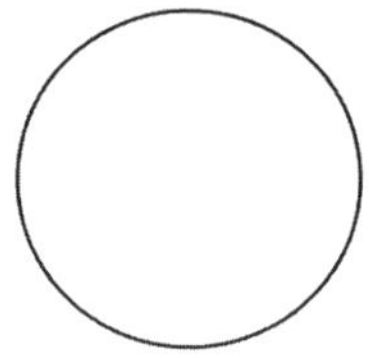

7. The one person, however, has two distinct natures—a divine nature and a human nature that are perfectly united.

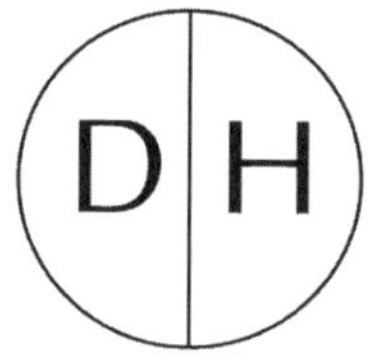

8. If the two natures were not united, the picture would look something like this—a divine nature and a human nature without any union—and that would be the Nestorian heresy.

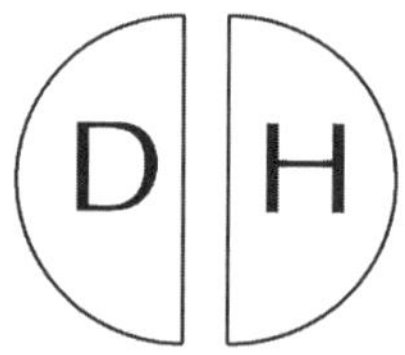

9. The circle represents the unity of the person, and the two halves represent the two natures, but the two natures are joined and united.

10. We don't know exactly how the two natures are united, but we do know that we do not want to say that they are united by way of a confusion of the two natures—the Monophysite heresy.

11. A problem that exists with the illustration as it stands is that by putting a circle here, some kind of limit or boundary is implied.
12. It is one thing to say that the human nature has boundaries or finite limits, but we encounter a problem if we put a boundary line on the side of the circle representing the divine nature.
13. A better way to picture that half of the circle would be with a dotted line.

14. The divine nature is united to the human nature, but this union does not mean that the divine nature is contained within finite boundaries.
15. The divine nature remains omnipresent and unlimited.

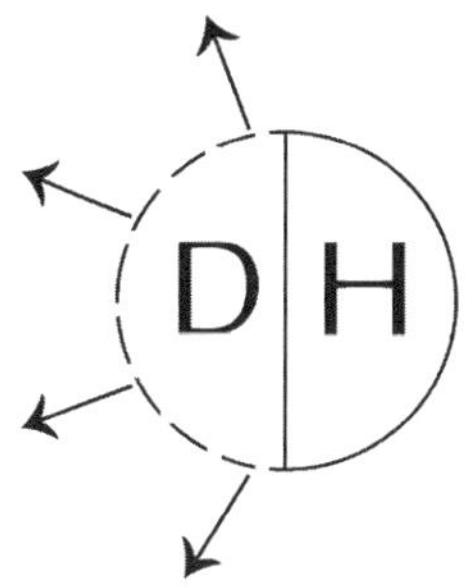

D. The Presence of the Human Nature in the Lord's Supper
   1. In the New Testament, Jesus talks about going away and about staying.
   2. He indicates that He will depart and does so at His ascension.
   3. Yet He also says to His disciples that He will be with them always.
   4. Even though the human nature ascended, the divine nature remains with the church.
   5. And even though the human nature is somewhere other than this world, it remains perfectly united to the divine nature, which can be everywhere.

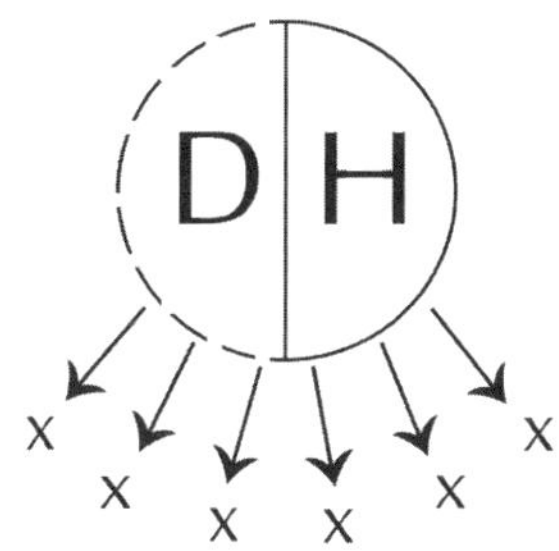

   6. When a person is in communion with the divine nature, he is in communion with the person of Christ and all that He is.
   7. When a person is in communion with the divine nature, he is in communion with the human nature, which is in perfect union with the divine nature.
   8. At no point is the human nature separated from the divine nature, so the person of Christ can be present at more than one place by virtue of the omnipresence of the divine nature even though the human nature remains localized in heaven.

STUDY QUESTIONS

1. Reformed believers often say that the Lutheran view of the presence of Christ is implicitly ____________.
   a. Eutychian
   b. Gnostic
   c. Nestorian
   d. Arian

2. The Latin phrase ___________ means,"The finite cannot contain the infinite."
   a. *Faculta se applicandi ad gratiam*
   b. *Fons totius divinitatis*
   c. *Fides filios Dei facit*
   d. *Finitum non capax infinitum*

BIBLE STUDY

1. Read the following texts of Scripture. What do they teach us about Jesus' presence with His people on earth?
   a. John 13:33
   b. John 14:28
   c. John 16:5
   d. John 16:7
   e. Acts 1:9
2. What does Jesus tell His disciples at the end of the Great Commission in Matthew 28:20? Can this statement be reconciled with the texts examined in question 1?
3. Lutherans argue that Reformed believers are implicitly Nestorian for denying that Christ's body and blood are physically present in the elements of the Lord's Supper. This argument is based on the Lutheran understanding of the communication of attributes and the ubiquity of the human nature of Christ. Since the union of the divine and human natures began at the incarnation, it would seem that this Lutheran argument would require Jesus' human nature to be ubiquitous from the point of His conception on. How does the Scripture speak of the human body of Christ? Does Scripture speak of Jesus as being in one place and not in another, or traveling from one locality to another? Does Scripture ever specifically say that Jesus' body is not present in a particular place (see Matthew 28:6)? Is the Lutheran criticism of Reformed believers supported by the biblical descriptions of Christ's body?

DISCUSSION QUESTIONS

1. Explain how Christ can be said to be present in the Lord's Supper without attributing ubiquity to His human nature.
2. Lutherans (and Roman Catholics) often accuse Reformed Christians of Nestorianism for denying that the divine attribute of omnipresence is communicated to the human nature of Christ. They argue that a refusal to grant the communication of attributes necessarily leads to Nestorianism and a division of Christ into two persons. Reformed Christians deny the charge and say that the Lutherans and Roman Catholics are violating Chalcedon. They could also say that the Lutherans and Roman Catholics are being inconsistent. Both the Lutherans and the Roman Catholics grant that ubiquity (or omnipresence) is not an inherent

attribute of human nature. Spatial finitude is an attribute of human nature. This is why the attribute of ubiquity must be communicated from the divine nature to the human nature according to their doctrine. Reformed Christians could potentially argue, however, that if the communication of attributes from one nature to the other is necessary to avoid Nestorianism, then there is no plausible reason why that communication should go in only one direction. If the divine attribute of omnipresence must be communicated to the human nature of Christ to avoid Nestorianism, then the human attribute of finitude must likewise be communicated to the divine nature to avoid Nestorianism. How would you evaluate the arguments on both sides of this debate? Does the doctrine of the communication of attributes contradict Chalcedon? Is the doctrine internally inconsistent?

APPLICATION

1. Have you ever considered what is happening when you partake of the bread and wine in the Lord's Supper? How will the things you have learned about the presence of Christ in the Supper affect the manner in which you partake of the sacrament?
2. Book 4, chapter 17 of Calvin's *Institutes of the Christian Religion* is a very helpful discussion of the doctrine of the Lord's Supper. Find an unabridged edition of this work (in a library or bookstore) and take the time to study it.

FOR FURTHER STUDY

Calvin, John. *Institutes of the Christian Religion*, 4.17

Letham, Robert. *The Lord's Supper*

Mathison, Keith. *Given for You: Reclaiming Calvin's Doctrine of the Lord's Supper*, chapters 7–8

Sproul, R.C. *What Is the Lord's Supper?*

7

Blessing and Judgment

MESSAGE INTRODUCTION

The nature of the mode of Christ's presence in the Supper has not been the only source of controversy in connection with this sacrament. The doctrine of transubstantiation resulted in the practice of adoring and worshiping the consecrated host—a practice that the Protestant Reformers found inherently idolatrous. The Roman Catholic doctrine of the sacrifice of the Mass was likewise rejected by the Reformers. In this lecture, Dr. Sproul explains these and other important controversies that surround the Lord's Supper.

LEARNING OBJECTIVES

1. To be able to explain how the doctrine of transubstantiation led to the practice of worshiping the host as well as why the Reformers rejected this practice
2. To be able to explain why the Reformers rejected the idea of the Lord's Supper as an unbloody repetition of Christ's sacrifice
3. To be able to explain why it is vitally important that Christians come to the Lord's Table with humility and repentance

QUOTATIONS

In this sacrament, Christ is not offered up to His Father; nor any real sacrifice made at all, for remission of sins of the quick or dead; but only a commemoration of that one offering up of Himself, by Himself, upon the cross, once for all: and a spiritual oblation of all possible praise unto God, for the same: so that the popish sacrifice of the mass (as they call it) is most abominably injurious to Christ's one, only sacrifice, the only propitiation for all the sins of His elect.

—Westminster Confession of Faith, 24.2

We shall benefit very much from the Sacrament if this thought is impressed and engraved upon our minds: that none of the brethren can be injured, despised, rejected, abused, or in any way offended by us, without at the same time, injuring, despising, and abusing Christ by the wrongs we do; that we cannot disagree with our brethren without at the same time disagreeing with Christ; that we cannot love Christ without loving him in the brethren; that we ought to take the same care of our brethren's bodies as we take of our own; for they are members of our body; and that, as no part of our body is touched by any feeling of pain which is not spread among all the rest, so we ought not to allow a brother to be affected by any evil, without being touched with compassion for him. Accordingly, Augustine with good reason frequently calls this Sacrament "the bond of love."

—John Calvin

LECTURE OUTLINE

A. Introduction

1. The disputes between the Roman Catholics and the Reformers and among the Reformers themselves were not limited to the christological concerns already discussed.
2. There were a host of other controversies.
3. One of Calvin's passionate concerns, for example, was to rid the church of any and all elements of idolatry, and this affected his doctrine of the Lord's Supper.

B. The Adoration of the Host

1. As we see from texts such as 1 Corinthians 10:14ff., the church has always had to struggle with the intrusion of idolatry into the liturgy of the church—particularly with respect to the Lord's Supper.
2. Calvin argued that the doctrine of transubstantiation involved one of the most subtle forms of idolatry there can be.
3. We worship the person of Christ, but we do not extrapolate the human nature from the divine and then worship the human nature.
4. To worship the human nature apart from the divine nature would be to worship the creature rather than the Creator.
5. Calvin and the other Reformers were concerned about the Roman Catholic practice of worshiping the consecrated host.
6. Not only is the consecrated host adored in the Roman Catholic Church, it is often elevated and carried about in processions.
7. In the eyes of Calvin and the other Reformers, all of these practices were inherently idolatrous.

C. The Sacrifice of the Mass

1. Another point of controversy centered on what actually occurred during the celebration of the Mass.
2. The Roman Catholic Church teaches that what happens in the Mass is the repetition of the sacrifice that Christ made upon the cross.
3. The sacrifice of the Mass is said to be an unbloody sacrifice, but nevertheless a real sacrifice.

4. The Reformers found this doctrine to be virtually blasphemous because it rejects what the book of Hebrews teaches—that Christ offered Himself once for all.

D. Blessing or Judgment

1. In 1 Corinthians 11:17–34, Paul gives the church a warning about the abuse of the Lord's Supper.
2. In the church at Corinth, the Lord's Supper had become an occasion for unbridled gluttony and selfishness.
3. The whole point of the Supper was being destroyed by this behavior.
4. Because of Paul's teaching here, one of the principles that came out of the Reformation is the practice of "fencing the table."
5. The purpose of fencing the table is not to exclude people but to protect those people who would partake of the Supper in an unworthy manner.
6. The consequence of such unworthy eating and drinking—*manducatio indignorum*—is that instead of having a cup of blessing they are having a cup of cursing and exposing themselves to the judgment of God.
7. Oscar Cullmann, the well-known twentieth-century biblical scholar, said that the most neglected verse in the whole New Testament is 1 Corinthians 11:30, which reads, "For this reason many are weak and sick among you, and many sleep."
8. Historically, this is one of the main reasons why most churches do not practice paedocommunion; they want to protect the children from participating in holy things they do not understand.
9. We are to come to the table with a certain amount of discernment, and we are to come with a proper attitude of humility and repentance.
10. In ourselves, all of us are unworthy to partake, but we come to commune with Christ precisely because of our need.

STUDY QUESTIONS

1. According to Dr. Sproul, which Reformer had a particularly strong concern to rid the church of any and all elements of idolatry?
   a. Martin Luther
   b. John Calvin
   c. Johannes Eck
   d. Thomas Cranmer

2. Which Roman Catholic practice, based on the doctrine of transubstantiation, did the Reformers believe to be idolatrous?
   a. The consecration of the host
   b. The elevation of the host
   c. The adoration of the host
   d. Both b and c

3. The Roman Catholic church teaches that the Mass is ___________.
   a. The symbolic memorial of Christ's sacrifice on the cross
   b. The sacrificial meal, to be distinguished but not separated from the act of sacrifice that Christ accomplished on the cross
   c. Merely a dramatic reenactment of Christ's sacrifice on the cross
   d. The actual repetition of the same sacrifice that Christ made upon the cross

4. Oscar Cullmann said that the most neglected verse in the whole New Testament is ___________.
   a. 1 Corinthians 11:30
   b. Matthew 1:3
   c. Romans 16:8
   d. 3 John 13

BIBLE STUDY

1. Read Matthew 26:26 and Mark 14:22. After Jesus takes the bread, blesses it, breaks it, and gives it to His disciples, what two things does He tell them to do with the bread? Does He tell them to genuflect before the bread and worship it? Is there any place in the New Testament that indicates that any of the first Christians worshiped the bread at the celebration of the Lord's Supper?
2. When a sacrificial meal was connected with a sacrifice in the Old Testament, the acts of sacrifice and the sacrificial meal were distinguished without being separated. The act of slaying the victim was the propitiatory sacrifice. The act of eating the sacrificial victim was the sacrificial meal, a means by which the benefits of the sacrifice were communicated to those who ate. As Calvin explained it, "after Christ's sacrifice was accomplished, the Lord instituted another method [the Lord's Supper] for us, that is, to transmit to the believing folk the benefit of the sacrifice offered to himself by his Son" (*Institutes*, 4.18.12). Read the laws concerning the peace offering in Leviticus 3 and 7 for an outline of the connection between a sacrifice and a sacrificial meal. Read Exodus 12. What indications are there that the Passover meal was a sacrificial meal?
3. Read 1 Corinthians 11:17–34. Based on what Paul says in this section of his letter, what is going on during the celebration of the Lord's Supper at the church in Corinth? How does Paul justify his condemnation of what is happening at Corinth? What does Paul tell the church to do in order to correct the situation?

DISCUSSION QUESTIONS

1. Explain how the doctrine of transubstantiation led to the practice of worshiping the consecrated host. What are some of the fundamental problems with this practice?
2. Why did the Reformers reject the idea that the Lord's Supper was an unbloody repetition of Christ's sacrifice?

3. How has your understanding of the Lord's Supper been affected by this series? Has your view been challenged? Strengthened? What is the most important thing that you have learned during the course of this series?

APPLICATION

1. Why is it vitally important to come to the Lord's Table with an attitude of repentance and humility? Have you previously failed to come to the table with this attitude? Each time you celebrate the Lord's Supper, take the time to prepare your heart beforehand.
2. Reflect on the words of John Calvin in the "Quotations" section above. Remember that since the Lord's Supper is a time of communion with Christ, it is therefore also a time of communion with all who are in Christ. In the time you set aside to prepare your heart for the sacrament, put away all bitterness, unforgiveness, and discord with your brothers and sisters in Christ.

FOR FURTHER STUDY

Calvin, John. *Institutes of the Christian Religion*, 4.17–18

Letham, Robert. *The Lord's Supper*

Mathison, Keith. *Given for You: Reclaiming Calvin's Doctrine of the Lord's Supper*, chapter 7

Sproul, R.C. *What Is the Lord's Supper?*

Warfield, B.B. "The Fundamental Significance of the Lord's Supper," *Selected Shorter Writings*, Vol. 1, pp. 332–38